Dealing With Waste

OLD APPLIANCES

Sally Morgan

Smart Apple Media

This book has been published in cooperation with Franklin Watts.

Editor: Rachel Minay, Designer: Brenda Cole, Picture research: Morgan Interactive Ltd., Consultant: Graham Williams

Published in the United States by Smart Apple Media
2140 Howard Drive West, North Mankato, Minnesota 56003

Library of Congress Cataloging-in-Publication Data

Morgan, Sally.
Old appliances / by Sally Morgan.
p. cm. — (Dealing with waste)
Includes index.
ISBN-13: 978-1-59920-012-5
1. Waste electronic apparatus and appliances—Recycling. I. Title.

TD799.85.M66 2007
363.72'88—dc22   2006035140

9 8 7 6 5 4 3 2 1

Contents

Electrical appliances

The modern world depends on electricity. Each day we use all kinds of electrical appliances, many of which are essential to a 21st-century way of life.

All kinds of electrical gadgets

Modern homes are full of electrical appliances. Kitchens have microwaves, refrigerators, freezers, washing machines, and dishwashers. There are electric mixers, juicers, and much more. Elsewhere in the home there are televisions with satellite boxes, computers, DVD players, video game consoles, and MP3 players.

Many people entertain themselves by watching television or playing video games.

It's my world!

People use many electrical items in their daily lives. Make a record of all the different ones that you use in one day. Which ones are essential and which ones could you do without?

Schools in the developed world, such as this one in the United States, are well equipped with computers so that each student in a class has access to one.

Using raw materials

Each year, the number of electrical appliances made throughout the world increases, and this uses up raw materials. Then the appliances are packaged and transported to shops to be sold to consumers. When they are put into use, they use electricity.

More waste

People create a lot of waste, including paper, glass, plastic, and garden clippings. The fastest growing type of waste is electrical waste. At the end of their lives, many electrical appliances are dumped with the garbage. This is a loss of valuable materials that could be recycled.

Making waste

Each year, people throw away huge quantities of electrical waste such as old televisions, refrigerators, computers, and cell phones. This may be because they no longer work or simply because they have been replaced by newer models. Much of this waste ends up in huge holes in the ground called landfills, but lots of it could be recycled instead.

Many electrical goods have been put in this dumpster for recycling. The metal parts are valuable and can be recycled over and over again.

Cost of repair

In the past, it was common to keep electrical appliances for a long time. This was partly because electrical appliances were more expensive to buy, compared with earnings. Also, electrical appliances were well-made, and they could be taken apart and repaired. Now it is often cheaper to throw something away and buy a new one. Many of the less expensive appliances are not designed to be repaired. For example, if an iron is dropped on the floor, the plastic may crack. This is difficult to repair, so there is no alternative but to replace it.

Keeping up-to-date

Some electrical appliances are replaced even when they are in perfect working order because they are no longer fashionable. For example, new models of cell phones and video game consoles are produced, and for some people, it is important to have the latest model.

It's my world!

Look at the electrical appliances in your home. How many are more than five years old? How many are less than one year old?

Did you know . . .

On average, electronic and electrical equipment make up four percent of European domestic waste, and this amount is growing three times faster than any other type of waste.

Business waste

Businesses create a lot of electrical waste, too, especially from computers. Computers are getting faster and more powerful all the time, so within a couple of years a computer or monitor can be out of date. For example, people are replacing the old bulky monitors—even though there is nothing wrong with them—with the latest flat-screen monitors because they take up less space on a desk.

This huge pile of old refrigerators and freezers is waiting to be recycled.

Reusing computers

The average life of a computer is just three years, and it is likely that this will fall within the next few years to be just one to two years. It is estimated that for every new computer that is purchased, another is thrown away. Nine out of every ten of these computers are in perfect working order.

Secondhand computers

Computers do not need to be thrown away. Computers that are in working order can be sold to other people or taken to shops that sell secondhand computers and accessories such as printers, CD writers, hard drives, and monitors. Also, there are companies that specialize in taking older computers and bringing them up-to-date by giving them faster processors or more memory.

It's my world!

Do you use a computer at school? Computers are an essential part of modern learning, but imagine what it would be like if your school did not have a computer. Find out what happens to the computers in your school when they are no longer required.

This computer workshop collects old computers. They are checked and repaired so they can be used again.

This warehouse is full of old computer monitors. Some will be sold, but others will be taken apart and recycled.

Computer aid

A business may not want a computer that is more than a few years old, but there are plenty of people in the world who would like to have the opportunity to own a computer. In many developing countries, 99 people out of every 100 do not have a computer, and most schools lack computers, too. There are charities that specialize in supplying computers to people in developing countries. Businesses can give their old computers to these charities, who will then check that the computers are in perfect working order before shipping them overseas.

Recycling computers

Although a few computers are reused, most are thrown away. In the past, computers and such components as printers, scanners, and cables all ended up in landfill sites. This is changing as governments pass laws that would require manufacturers to take computers back once the machines have been used up.

Valuable metals

Computers may look as if they are made mostly of plastic, but there is a significant amount of metal inside the circuit board and hard drive. An old-style computer monitor and its circuit board together contain about 6.6 pounds (3 kg) of lead, which is valuable, but also harmful. In addition, there are smaller amounts of gold, mercury, cadmium, copper, chromium, and arsenic, many of which are also harmful. Computers have to be taken apart and recycled carefully to make sure the dangerous materials do not leak out or poison the person doing the recycling.

These connectors contain plastic and metal, which can be extracted and recycled.

These computer circuit boards have been cut up and made into clipboards and key rings.

It's my world!

More than 375 million printer cartridges are thrown away each year worldwide. What do you do with the old cartridges from a printer? When you open the packaging for a cartridge, check inside to see if there are any instructions about recycling it. Some companies provide a postage-paid envelope in which you can send the cartridge for recycling. Some organizations collect used cartridges and raise money for charity. Sometimes you can take your old cartridge to a store to be refilled.

Recycling cartridges

A printer cartridge is mostly plastic and aluminum, which can be recycled. The large toner cartridges for a laser printer or a photocopier can be reused. They are completely dismantled and cleaned, any worn parts are replaced, and the drum is either re-coated or replaced. They are then refilled with fresh toner, tested, and sold with a guarantee.

Cell phones

The number of cell phones in the world is increasing rapidly. In 2005, an estimated 780 million cell phones were sold around the world. This creates a lot of potential waste for the future.

Hazardous materials

Cell phones contain metals such as platinum, gold, silver, and copper, and hazardous materials such as cadmium. These materials are completely harmless in the phone, but if they are dumped into a landfill, they can leak into the ground and pollute water sources. For example, the cadmium from one cell phone battery is enough to pollute 158,500 gallons (600,000 l) of water. Therefore, cell phones have to be disposed of safely rather than thrown away. Stores that sell cell phones have collection points for old phones. Some allow you to trade in your old phone when you buy a new one.

Having the latest model of a cell phone is important to some people, and they replace their phones regularly.

Old cell phones can be valuable. There are groups that raise money for charity by recycling cell phones. See if your school could start collecting cell phones to raise money for new equipment or for a local charity.

Many cell phone stores collect old cell phones and send them to be recycled.

Recycling a phone

Any cell phones that are in good condition can be sent to developing countries to be reused. They may not be the latest models, but they work well. Older models have to be recycled. The phones are taken apart, and the battery is recycled separately. The plastic casing is removed and broken into small crumbs called granules. These can be sent to manufacturers that use recycled plastic. The plastic from cell phones can be used for many things, such as making traffic cones and artificial surfaces for playgrounds and sports facilities. The metal parts can also be melted down and recycled.

Batteries

Batteries are used to power items such as laptop computers, cell phones, clocks, toys, cameras, and much more. These kinds of items use dry-cell batteries. They are small and convenient, but millions are thrown away each year.

The dry batteries that are used to power toys, video game consoles, and other electrical items have to be replaced regularly.

Types of batteries

There are different types of dry-cell batteries. Most batteries are the type that is used once and thrown away. They contain chemicals such as zinc chloride, mercuric oxide, or silver oxide. Another type of battery is a rechargeable battery, which can be used over and over again because it can be recharged using electricity. These batteries contain chemicals such as nickel, cadmium, or lithium. It is better to use rechargeable batteries because this reduces the number of batteries that need to be bought and then thrown away.

Did you know . . .

▶ Each year, Americans buy about 3.5 billion batteries—or about 32 batteries per family. Australians discard about 8,800 tons (8,000 t) of used batteries each year.

▶ The energy needed to make a battery is 50 times greater than the energy it gives out.

Recycling batteries

Batteries should be recycled rather than put in the trash. Sometimes there are special recycling locations for batteries. The different types have to be recycled separately because they contain different chemicals such as cadmium and mercury, which are harmful. The metal that forms the case of the battery can also be recycled. Most batteries are recycled by heating, which causes the metal to melt and separate out. The metals can then be made into new batteries or other items.

It's my world!

What can you do?

▸ Use electricity rather than a battery whenever possible.

▸ Use rechargeable batteries and a battery charger.

▸ Try to use rechargers that are powered from a small solar panel or from a wind-up mechanism; for example, there are some wind-up cell phone chargers.

▸ Dispose of all your batteries safely by taking them to battery recycling locations.

▸ Send batteries back to manufacturers for recycling or reprocessing if possible.

Dangerous waste

If batteries end up in landfill sites, they may start to leak. The chemicals seep into the ground and may be carried by water into local streams. This can poison fish and other aquatic animals.

This dry battery has ended up on the seabed. The chemicals in the battery will leak out into the water and could harm nearby marine life.

Fridges and freezers

A refrigerator is an essential piece of equipment in the kitchen because it keeps food fresh for longer. In recent years, the number of refrigerators and freezers in the world has increased as more people can afford to buy them. There are very few homes in Australia, Europe, or North America without a refrigerator or freezer.

A lot of raw materials are used to make a large refrigerator, including metals, plastic, and coolant. These can all be recycled.

Inside a refrigerator

Refrigerators and freezers have an outer casing made of metal or plastic and an insulating wall of foam. The inside is covered in plastic so it can be wiped clean. All refrigerators and freezers contain a coolant. This is a liquid that circulates within the appliance. It keeps the inside cool by taking heat from the inside and releasing it to the outside.

It's my world!

A refrigerator uses electricity to stay cool. There are ways to minimize the use of electricity. Refrigerators should never be placed near an oven, as the heat from the oven makes the refrigerator work much harder. Check the temperature setting of the refrigerator. There is no need to have it on the coldest setting unless the weather is very warm. Do not continuously open the refrigerator because cool air escapes each time. Also, do not place hot foods in the refrigerator. Leave them out until they have cooled down.

CFCs

In the past, the coolant used in refrigerators was a chemical called CFC or chloroflurocarbon. This chemical was used widely in all forms of refrigeration equipment, fire extinguishers, air conditioning units, and aerosols. It was also used in the foam lining of refrigerators. Then it was discovered that CFCs were destroying ozone gases high in the atmosphere. The ozone layer is important because it absorbs harmful ultraviolet light in sunlight. The ozone had to be protected, so during the 1990s, most countries banned the manufacture of CFCs and related chemicals. More recently it has been discovered that CFCs are also greenhouse gases, and they contribute to global warming. There are many refrigerators and freezers that contain CFCs still in existence, and they have to be disposed of carefully.

The ozone layer is thinning over Antarctica. The levels of ozone have been measured, and this photo shows the results. The dark blue area shows where the ozone layer is thinnest.

19

Reusing and recycling fridges

Some unwanted refrigerators and freezers can be reused. There are companies that take old appliances and refurbish them so they can be resold. They drain any CFCs and replace them with a safe alternative. Then they check that the appliance works and resell it.

Secondhand use

New refrigerators and freezers are expensive in many developing countries, and people cannot afford to buy them. As a result, there is a need for second-hand refrigerators and freezers from developed countries. The CFCs are removed by specialist refrigeration companies and replaced with a different coolant before the refrigerator or freezer is exported.

In some countries, refrigerators that no longer work are taken apart, and people use the spare parts to repair other refrigerators.

Does it contain CFC?

Most refrigerators are marked with an "appliance rating plate." This is a metal plate or sticky label on the back of the appliance. The plate contains information about the appliance such as the model, serial number, and the type of coolant it uses. Refrigerators that are marked with R12 or R134a on the plate will probably have CFC or HCFC in the insulation foam and will need special treatment when the refrigerator is recycled.

Did you know . . .

As many as 3 million domestic refrigerators and freezers are disposed of each year in the United Kingdom (UK). Of these, 90 percent are recycled.

The metal casing of a refrigerator is shredded and poured into bags. This makes it easier to transport the metal to factories where it will be recycled.

The recycling process

In some countries, laws prevent refrigerators and freezers from being dumped in landfills. If a refrigerator or freezer cannot be repaired, it must be recycled. About 90 percent of a refrigerator can be recycled. The CFC is drained out and usually burned. Any CFC in the foam insulation is also removed and burned. Then the external case and things such as shelves are stripped out.

This leaves a white box, which is shredded. The bags of shredded refrigerators contain different materials, such as metal and different plastics, which are separated and recycled. The plastics can be sent to factories that make new goods—such as plant pots, boots, and garden furniture—from recycled plastic. Metals can be melted down and shaped into a wide range of new objects.

Electric lights

Homes are lit up by a variety of light bulbs, such as tungsten lights, low-energy bulbs, and fluorescent tubes. There are lots of lights on streets, too. When they come to the end of their lives, they are thrown away. Fluorescent tubes in particular need to be disposed of carefully because they contain mercury, a poisonous chemical.

One way to reduce waste is to replace traditional bulbs with low-energy bulbs, which do not need to be replaced as often.

It's my world!

Look at the electrical lights in your home. You may be surprised by how many there are. Are any of them fluorescent lights? Do you know if there are any low-energy bulbs? How could you reduce the amount of electricity that is used by lights in your home?

Low-energy bulbs

Tungsten filament bulbs used in the home have to be replaced regularly, and most end up in the garbage. These bulbs are not usually recycled, although the metals inside could be melted down. A better alternative is to use a long-lasting low-energy bulb. Not only do these bulbs use far less electricity, but they last longer, so fewer need to be thrown away.

Did you know . . .

As many as 500 million fluorescent lamps are dumped in landfills in the U.S. every year. These lamps may contain as much as four tons (3.6 t) of mercury. Mercury is so dangerous that the mercury from one fluorescent tube can pollute 7,925 gallons (30,000 l) of water beyond a safe level for drinking.

Fluorescent tubes

Fluorescent tubes can be recycled. The tubes are taken to a recycling facility where the main components of glass, metal, and mercury are separated. The tube has to be taken apart carefully to make sure the mercury vapor does not escape.

This man is wearing protective clothing and a breathing apparatus because he is taking old fluorescent tubes apart, and they contain mercury. He is pushing the tube into a machine that removes the mercury vapor.

Recycling packaging

Electrical goods are sold with lots of packaging. For example, a new refrigerator is packed in polystyrene foam and wrapped in plastic inside a cardboard case. This packaging is needed to protect the goods during transportation, but it should not be thrown away because much of it can be recycled.

Recycling cardboard

Cardboard can be shredded, mixed with water, and stirred until it breaks down into individual fibers. Foreign objects, such as staples and bits of tape, are removed using filters. The clean pulp is passed through a series of rollers. This flattens it and removes any remaining water.

Making cardboard from recycled pulp uses about 75 percent of the energy used in the manufacture of cardboard from new pulp. However, each time cardboard is recycled, the fibers become weaker, limiting the number of times it can be recycled. This

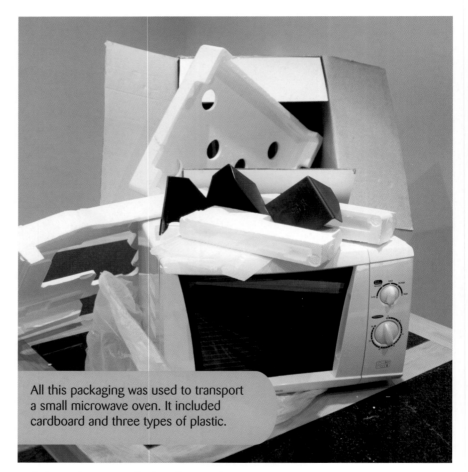

All this packaging was used to transport a small microwave oven. It included cardboard and three types of plastic.

is usually about eight times. To avoid this, the recycled pulp is often mixed with new pulp. Cardboard can also be recycled to make paper towels, tissues, newsprint, and writing paper.

A stack of cardboard boxes has been collected for recycling from a market in this Chinese town.

It's my world!

The next time your family buys an electrical appliance make sure that as much of the packaging as possible is recycled. Cardboard can usually be taken to local recycling centers. Look to see if the cardboard is made from recycled material already. This will be indicated by a triangular recycling symbol with a number in the middle that represents the percentage of recycled paper. Some recycling centers take polystyrene packaging, too.

Polystyrene

The polystyrene foam can be recycled, too. Polystyrene is identified by a symbol stamped onto its surface. It is a triangle with the number 6 in the middle. Polystyrene is taken to factories where it is washed, flaked, dried, and squeezed into recycled polystyrene pellets. The pellets are melted down and made into new polystyrene objects.

The way ahead

There are many ways of tackling the problem of increasing electrical waste. They include extending the life of the product, making it more energy efficient so it uses less electricity, and encouraging more recycling.

Longer product life

If electrical appliances had a longer life, people would not have to buy so many. One way to move forward could be for manufacturers to extend the warranty period, the period during which the manufacturer repairs the appliance free of charge. It has been proven that extended warranty periods encourage consumers to keep an appliance for longer. Electrical appliances also need to be easy to dismantle and repair. This can be improved at the design stage of the product.

This sculpture is made from 3.3 tons (3 t) of electrical waste. It includes 5 refrigerators, 35 cell phones, 5 toasters, and 4 lawnmowers. Its teeth are made from computer mice, its spine from a washing machine, and its neck from a vacuum cleaner.

Using less electricity

Electrical appliances use a lot of electricity, and most electricity is generated using coal, oil, or gas. These fuels create polluting gases when they are burned. An energy-efficient appliance is one that is designed to do its job using the minimum amount of electricity. If people bought energy-efficient appliances and fitted low-energy light bulbs, the demand for electricity would decrease. It would be even better if electricity could be generated using renewable energy from the sun or wind.

Recycling everything

The amount of electrical waste can be reduced if everybody makes sure that all old electrical appliances, batteries, and printer cartridges are recycled.

It's my world!

What can you do?

▸ Turn off electric appliances such as televisions, computers, and lights when they are not in use to save electricity. Many people leave televisions, DVDs, and computers on "standby," but this just wastes electricity.

▸ Use rechargeable batteries.

▸ Try to keep cell phones, video game consoles, and similar items for as long as possible. When you decide to upgrade, make sure the old one is handed on to somebody else or is recycled.

▸ Recycle all the packaging that comes with a new electrical appliance.

Turn off lights and electrical appliances when they are not in use.

Glossary

Appliance
a household device operated by electricity or gas

Battery
a device that stores electricity

CFC (chloroflurocarbon)
a chemical used in refrigeration that is harmful to the ozone layer

Coolant
a fluid that is used to carry heat away from something

Developed country
a country in which most people have a high standard of living

Developing country
a country in which most people have a low standard of living and poor access to goods and services compared with people in a developed country

Efficiency
a measure of how much energy something uses in order to carry out its function; for example, an energy-efficient refrigerator will use less electricity to keep food chilled than a less efficient refrigerator

Global warming
the gradual warming of the average temperature of Earth, caused by an increase in greenhouse gases

Greenhouse gas
a gas in the atmosphere that traps heat

Landfill
a large hole in the ground used to dispose of waste

Ozone layer
a layer high in Earth's atmosphere that contains the gas ozone (a form of oxygen) and absorbs harmful ultraviolet rays from the sun

Pollute
to release harmful materials into the environment

Recycle
to process and reuse materials in order to make new items

Reduce
to lower the amount of waste produced

Reuse
to use something again, either in the same way or in a different way

Tungsten
a chemical element that is used to make electric light filaments

Waste
anything that is thrown away, abandoned, or released into the environment in a way that could harm the environment

Web sites

Cell Phone Recycling
www.grerecycling.com
Learn about cell phone recycling and fundraising at the Web site.

Container Recycling Institute
www.container_recycling.org
Click on the "Just for Kids" link to find fun recycling activities.

Earth 911
www.earth911.org/master.asp
This Web site shows a variety of national and local U.S. recycling programs and events.

Freecycle
www.freecycle.com
Web site where members can send e-mails to other members of the group listing items that they want to recycle free of charge rather than dumping on a landfill site.

Friendly Packaging
http://friendlypackaging.org.uk/novel.htm
Web site about the different types of materials that are used in packaging and how they can be recycled.

Friends of the Earth
www.foe.org.uk
Web site of the charity Friends of the Earth that gives information about environmental campaigns, including those for encouraging recycling and against incinerators and landfills.

Let's Recycle
www.letsrecycle.com/index.jsp
Web site looking at all sorts of waste and how it can be recycled.

U.S. Environmental Protection Agency
www.epa.gov
This Web site has lots of environmental information on all issues, not just waste. There is an EPA Kids Club (www.epa.gov/kids) with information on waste and recycling.

Waste Wise
www.wastewise.wa.gov.au/pages/recycling.asp
An Australian Web site with information about how to recycle anything and everything.

Index

DATE DUE

Demco, Inc. 38-293